D1604052

Trauma
Recovery

You Are A Winner

A New Choice Through
Natural Developmental Movements

SVETLANA MASGUTOVA PH.D.

PAMELA CURLEE

1st WORLD PUBLISHING

Trauma Recovery—You Are A Winner

☺

Svetlana Masgutova Ph.D. & Pamela Curlee

© Svetlana Masgutova Ph.D. & Pamela Curlee 2007

Published by 1stWorld Publishing
1100 North 4th St. Fairfield, Iowa 52556
tel: 641-209-5000 • fax: 641-209-3001
web: www.1stworldpublishing.com

First printed in 2004

LCCN: 2007924921
SoftCover ISBN: 978-1-4218-9954-1
HardCover ISBN: 978-1-4218-9955-8
eBook ISBN: 978-1-4218-9956-5

This material has been written and published solely for educational purposes. The authors and the publisher shall have neither liability nor responsibility to any person or entity with respect to any loss, damage or injury caused or alleged to be caused directly or indirectly by the information contained in this book.

The information included in these pages about the movement-based learning system known as Educational Kinesiology, including the Brain Gym activities, derives from the published works of Paul E. Dennison and Gail E. Dennison and is used by permission. Brain Gym® is a registered trademark of the Educational Kinesiology Foundation/Brain Gym® International, www.braingym.org and edukfd@earthlink.net; (800) 356-2109 from the U.S.A. and Canada and (805) 658-7942 from all other countries. The Brain Gym® trademark is used herein by permission of Brain Gym® International

Editors: Sonia Nordenson, JoEllen Firestone.
Photography: Dr. Svetlana Masgutova, Kim Sadikov
Drawing of Tiananmen Square: Dr. Paul Curlee
Braneland story: Ericka Curlee
Brain Gym photo models: Rylee Fuentes, Bryce Lowry, Garrett Lowry, Hayden Lowry

TABLE OF CONTENTS

Foreword. 7

Preface 9

Introduction 15

1 Madness and Despair. 19

2 The Children on the Train. 21

3 June 4, 1989 23

4 Joining the Team in Ufa. 31

5 The Thousands Who Came to Help 35

6 An Unprecedented Situation 39

7 Consulting the Little Orange Book 41

8 "Nikolai, You Are a Winner" 47

9 Alleviating Pain and Fear 51

10 Miracles Happen 55

11 Two-Handed Rainbows 59

12 Regaining Self-Worth. 63

13 Natural Developmental Movements. 65

14 A Resource for Happiness 71

15 The Epilogue. 73

16 The Theory Behind the Interventions at Ufa. 79

17 Moving Beyond Survival 87

18 An Allegorical Tale. 91

19 You, Too, Are a Winner. 103

20 About the Authors. 105

FOREWORD

Our innate, developmental movement patterns, together with the learned ones, are the "maps" we have in our DNA and in our experiential memory. We depend on these charts for movement in the world, and when we access them, we find our way to new learning and to living life to its fullest. The Brain Gym program activates these organizing and centralizing movements, ideally experienced by all humans as they progress from infancy to the stage of readiness for schooling. This is why people of all ages who do these specialized movements become more focused, aware, and self-initiating.

When Dr. Carla Hannaford initially handed her a copy of the original *Brain Gym®* book (written by my wife, Gail, and myself), Dr. Svetlana Masgutova knew little about our learning system. Though at first skeptical of the book's simplicity, Dr. Masgutova used its safe, easy-to-learn movements with children who had survived a devastating train wreck in Russia. In this way, she saw for herself some extraordinary evidence of the restorative benefits offered by the Brain Gym activities.

I vividly remember the letter Dr. Masgutova wrote to Gail and me in 1989, describing her experiences with the Brain Gym movements at the Ural hospital. Today, Svetlana is our dear friend and has been a colleague and an International Faculty member of the Educational Kinesiology Foundation for Russia and Poland. I'm grateful for her field research and for her collaboration with Pamela Curlee in the sharing of her results.

In this book, Masgutova and Curlee offer us a remarkable account of how children experiencing the aftermath of severe trauma learned to use the power of movement to redefine themselves beyond their immediate concerns. *Trauma Recovery—You Are A Winner* is a story of one person's vision to see beyond the apparent—beyond pain, horror, and suffering—and into the hearts and unseen possibilities of young people at a turning point. Most of all, it is a story of courage in the face of grief and loss—the courage to draw out the emerging individual in each child by trusting natural movement to activate the brain and neuropathways beyond survival and toward growth.

All of our life experiences—from those that are inspirational and triumphant to those that pose survival challenges—contribute to who we ultimately become. And movement (by this I mean conscious movement) truly is the door to learning. If we are to transcend our limiting survival patterns, we must (each and every one of us) heed the call to return to the body—to engage the eyes, ears, hands, feet, and sensory perception—in order to wake up the whole brain. Thank you, Svetlana, for sharing your understanding of the role of the primitive reflexes in protecting us and for reminding us of the need for movement to create the sense of self. I salute your work, as well as Pamela's understanding of Brain Gym and her skills of expression, and I recommend this book to readers everywhere.

Paul E. Dennison, Ph.D.
Ventura, California

PREFACE

Those who say it can't be done should not interrupt the person doing it.

—Chinese proverb

I have known Dr. Svetlana Masgutova since 1994. From time to time, she would humbly mention that she had helped with the psychological recovery of children who survived a train accident in central Russia. She would then move on to another subject as if the whole story had been told in that one thought. For years, I awaited the rest of the story.

Thank goodness she has decided it is time to go back and bravely open the door on those haunting memories so that the message of *Trauma Recovery—You Are a Winner* can now emerge into the world. This story confirms that the Brain Gym program is useful and important in our lives because it is based on the principles of natural learning. Dramatically, as demonstrated in the aftermath of this disaster, Brain Gym has sometimes also made the difference between life and death itself.

Svetlana's story points out the value and critical importance of movement and purposeful touch as catalysts for new learning and development. As schools stray further and further away from the natural, innate processes that enrich learning, it becomes clear why levels of academic frustration are often higher than the scores on academic tests. The children in Svetlana's story teach us that movement is fundamental to natural learning. Paradoxically, most educational systems put an obsessive emphasis on test preparation and performance while simultaneously expecting students to remain still and quiet. This approach is analogous to giving a toddler very clear instructions to stay immobile and just listen quietly while the procedures for learning how to walk are explained. True learning is facilitated and enriched by participation, movement, and experience.

A key message of this story is that the body is as involved with learning as the mind. In addition, the survivors of this tragedy have taught us that learning is severely hampered if the body doesn't feel safe. Ultimately, the children have demonstrated that getting in touch with the physical experience of safety allows for dynamic growth of the emotions and intellect.

This book shares the story of Svetlana's personal experience and summarizes how something so simple as the Brain Gym movements can be so profound. It is my intention that the message of this book should inspire us all. It should invite us to investigate the efficiency of the enriched learning that occurs when purposeful movements such as Brain Gym are introduced. Even though this particular story is extreme, the benefits of Brain Gym continue to be documented around the world in everyday enrichment of education, counseling, sports, business, and personal relationships. Movement is a critical key to the learning of new behavior, new attitudes, and new concepts.

While researching this book, I reviewed numerous newspapers from the days following the train accident and found that it was not an isolated event. It was amazing to me that millions of people all over the world were simulta-  neously being swept by the shock waves of a number of tragedies that struck the planet within forty-eight hours of time.

Because of the epidemic of catastrophes occurring within hours, millions of people worldwide were engaged in a simultaneous struggle with the mental and physiological experience of grief. Fear was spreading through the citizenries of numerous countries. The voice of mankind was calling out for relief from the pain and suffering of post-traumatic stress.

I was particularly struck by the fact that the famous photo of the student standing in front of the tanks at Tiananmen Square was on the front page of the same papers that carried the news of the tragic accident in Russia. One unarmed Chinese civilian painted a clear symbolic picture of what courage looks like. The young man stood alone, facing and thereby halting the progress of a column of tanks heading to Tiananmen Square. He not only stopped the movement of the tanks, he even climbed on the lead tank and spoke to its crew before friends pulled him away. It became clear to me that this photo, being sent around the world through the Associated Press, was a metaphor for our book.

Like the boy who stopped the movement of tanks in Tiananmen Square, Svetlana Masgutova models an inner strength that can confront the fear and madness that accompanies individual and global crisis and demand, "Stop!" The choice presented by tragedy is to either collapse under the weight of shock and fear or boldly stand before it and meet the crisis face to face. We then can begin moving into growth and development.

Svetlana found a successful way to help the children draw out clarity, inner strength, and courage from within. Later, she and I both used Brain Gym to meet personal tragedies, as well. It is with gratitude that we now share the same gift with you. Please pass it forward.

Pamela Curlee
Denver, Colorado

ACKNOWLEDGMENTS

How can the heart find words when its only language is love and gratitude?

◎ Love and gratitude to all the children of the catastrophe, who taught us all how to move through and beyond survival. Their courage, strength, and wisdom will continue to be an inspiration for many years to come.

◎ Love and gratitude to the Sadikovs, dearest parents of Svetlana, who have always been inspirational teachers and loving supporters. They assisted in gathering information and photographs regarding the catastrophe from witnesses, newspapers, and official reports.

◎ Love and gratitude to Denis Masgutov, Svetlana's dear son, for his unconditional patience in waiting for hours each day for her to return home from the hospital. His smile, open heart, and encouragement gave daily support and strength.

◎ Love and gratitude to Peter Hawryluk, Svetlana's husband, for all his support and his co-teaching of how survival and the feeling of safety can be turned into the drawing out of potential development. Thanks also to Peter for taking the pictures of the Brain Gym movements.

◎ Love and gratitude to the chief doctor of Ulu-Teliak Hospital, Nikolaj V. Jermoluk, for sharing his experience of the tragedy and for saving so many lives.

◎ Love and gratitude to Professor Vadim Safin, Svetlana's first teacher in psychology, for his psychological collaboration during the days following the accident.

☺ Love and gratitude to all of Svetlana's colleagues at the Bashkir State Education University, where she worked for four years at the beginning of her professional career.

☺ Love and gratitude to Natalia Tolstych for her encouragement to take the *Brain Gym®* book to Ufa.

☺ Love and gratitude to Dr. Paul Dennison and Gail Dennison for creating the Brain Gym material, which has awakened the *winner* inside of thousands of people around the world.

☺ Love and gratitude to Dr. Carla Hannaford for being one of the key pioneers who took Brain Gym to many different countries of the world while sharing its scientific effects. Taking the little orange *Brain Gym®* book to Moscow and writing about this work in her book *Smart Moves: Why Learning Is Not All in Your Head* has opened up the field of all possibilities to people around the globe.

☺ Love and gratitude to Tawni Lawrence for her dearest friendship and support in the manifestation of the vision of this book.

☺ Love and gratitude to Gail Dennison, Marilyn Lugaro, Barbara Sowada, and Cam Vuksinich for their contributions and creative ideas. Gratitude also to Dr. Paul Curlee for his drawing of Tiananmen Square.

☺ Love and gratitude to Pamela's beautiful and creative daughters, Ericka and Alexi Curlee, for their endless support and assistance. Deep gratitude to Ericka for major contributions to the story of "Braneland" and for hours of editing ideas.

☺ Love and gratitude to JoEllen Firestone and Sonia Nordenson for their professional editing skills.

☺ Love and gratitude to all the children who are pictured in this book: Oskar Bugajsky, Rylee Fuentes, and Bryce, Garrett, and Hayden Lowry.

INTRODUCTION

In 1989 I worked as a volunteer psychologist after a historic train catastrophe that occurred in the Ural Mountains of Russia. Immediately following the accident, I went to a children's ward in the city of Ufa in order to support the psychological recovery of numerous children who had been injured in this tragedy. My experience of working with the survivors of the accident significantly changed my professional and personal life.

Public interest in this story was stimulated by references in several professional journals and books, including a note in Dr. Carla Hannaford's book *Smart Moves: Why Learning Is Not All in Your Head*. For many years I have been asked by numerous people to write about my experiences. My main reason for sharing this story now is to tell the world the importance of Brain Gym, created by Dr. Paul Dennison and Gail Dennison. I know that all trauma survivors would also benefit greatly from this knowledge.

Somehow the courage to work with the psychological recovery of these young burn victims seemed to come naturally to me. It was so important to be in the present moment with these children as they struggled to survive. I simply volunteered for a task that had to be done.

For weeks after I left Ufa, the thoughts and memories of the children dying or caught in the grip of shock or panic would persistently return to my awareness. I would be walking down city streets, these memories flashing pictures in my mind again and again, and my eyes would flood with tears. My body would shake and sometimes freeze in response to the images. At other times my internal survival mechanism protected me by hiding the thoughts and memories from me because they were too much to bear. The memories of children with burned skin and damaged breathing systems were difficult to endure. In truth, my heart was silent, and at times it felt as if it were made of stone. I initially chose to set aside the details of this story, and I locked away the pictures in my desk and in my mind. I needed time. In this way I discovered the importance of the recovery mechanisms following any crisis. I personally experienced how efficiently nature has created strategies for survival. This led to my discovery and understanding of the bridge between being a survivor and being a *winner*.

Have you ever asked yourself in the aftermath of tragedy if you were a victim or were blessed by fortune? Do you know a way to move beyond a crisis? Do you find yourself stuck or moving chaotically? How do you experience your emotional response to surviving a shock or trauma?

Tragedy is not given to diminish us but to open new possibilities. It is given to us so that we might tap our endless resources of resilience. In traumatic times we often ask ourselves why this experience "happened to me." Based on my own history as well as on witnessing the misfortunes of others, I have found that an inherent part of human nature does not agree that we are meant to be victims. We were not born to suffer. We instinctively know this from our day of birth. This truth is encoded in our DNA, and needs only to be reawakened.

Pamela Curlee and I now want to share some new discoveries of the four-step process of true survival. The *winner* inside of anyone can carve a path in the midst of tragedy that becomes the road to happiness and joy, created by the experience of inner strength, courage, and wisdom.

In Singapore I met a four-year-old boy who philosophically told me in conversation, "Life is not perfect."

I was amazed by his level of intelligence, and cried out in response, "What?"

Looking disappointed, he commented that adults do not seem to understand this statement. I replied, "Oh no, you are absolutely right! I just didn't expect to hear this from a child." I added, "You are right, but we always have choices: Life may not seem perfect, and we can choose to do nothing; or life may not seem perfect, and we can choose to do many things to make it better."

The young boy jumped in excitement. "Oh yes, I never thought about having choice! It's a wonderful idea."

Our experiences are not endured for the sake of survival only. They also serve as motivation to experience deeper and more creative learning and understanding. I now feel the importance of sharing this story. My intent is not to frighten people with the details of this event but to share an effective way in which we can all move beyond the initial role of survivor and find the inner world of the *winner*. It's in every one of us!

Dr. Svetlana Masgutova
Warsaw, Poland

1. MADNESS AND DESPAIR

The moment I walked into the first room at the children's ward and saw the depth of despair before me, I realized that everything I had ever learned was now being turned upside down.

Madness. That is all there was. I was surrounded by madness, by a situation bigger and more drastic than anything I had ever seen or imagined.

How could I reach these tormented boys and girls? No one should have to endure such suffering. The children desperately needed my help, and I certainly had knowledge, yet I could not think of anything that could reach them in their present state.

Despite all my years of training, teaching, and experience, I had no guidance for a situation such as this. How could this be? I frantically scanned my memory banks, reviewing my logical and systematic training, and found nothing that would help these children.

But then, this situation wasn't logical, so why should I expect to find a logical solution? I needed to do something new and different—something I'd never done before. What was it? Where was it? All I wanted to do was reach out with compassion and assist the children in finding ways to be released from their bonds of suffering and pain.

I remember thinking to myself: *Sh-h-h-h! Be quiet, mind. Just listen. I will learn what to do. The children will help teach me. We must teach one another how to move through and beyond this catastrophe. I will teach them, they will teach me, and together we'll find a way for them to move beyond survival.*

So come, children, join me now and help me share this tale, so that others may learn what you have to teach us. Come, children, and help me find the words to let others know how to face a tragedy, how to sift through the shattered pieces of a life and find the hero who was always there.

You, my children, are *winners*. We must tell others how to discover this truth that lies within them, as well. There are natural, simple, proven methods that make all the difference for survival and eventually for the growth and development of who we can become. The secret lies within us, and it involves awakening our natural intelligence. The time has come to tell our story.

2. THE CHILDREN ON THE TRAIN

I remember hearing stories about the children who were on one of the trains. Many were on the journey because they had excelled in school and had won a vacation as an award for outstanding creativity, talent, and success in their studies. They had put in hours of schoolwork that had finally paid off and were filled with excitement and enthusiasm for this trip to their favorite retreat. With all the necessary preparations made, many had boarded at the train station in Novosibirsk. Their anticipation had built as they eagerly awaited the arrival of

A summer day at the Black Sea

the train that would carry them from the forests of Siberia to the holiday camp at Artek on the Crimea, where they would be able to enjoy the warm sun on the shores of the Black Sea.

The train had finally arrived, and the children had then eagerly boarded, some waving to family members who were seeing them off. Others boarded with parents, grandparents, and siblings who had elected to join in this journey of celebration. The train, consisting of twenty cars, also carried other families heading to the city of Adler near Sochi on the Black Sea Coast.

Another train was returning from the Black Sea. Its seventeen cars were filled with families returning from their vacations. These travelers had enjoyed their restful times, and were carrying memories of days at the beach: the food, the sun, the play, and the friendships shared. As the train gently swayed along the tracks in rhythmical movement, taking everyone back home, its passengers talked and shared stories.

One train was running behind schedule. Because it had left the station late, the two trains were destined to pass one another as they traveled through the forest 750 miles southeast of Moscow. Both trains traveled swiftly toward a picturesque valley near the town of Asha, nestled in the Ural Mountains of the Bashkir region of Russia. Most of the passengers on both trains had settled in for the night, feeling relaxed and content, and sleeping as best one can on a train.

A Soviet army officer was standing at the window of one train when he noticed an acrid smell. He later reported, "I sensed that something must be wrong, but before I could do anything, there was a glow and then a thunderous explosion."

It would be days before the actual cause of the catastrophe became known.

3. JUNE 4, 1989

Disasters are always unexpected. I initially heard reports of a railway catastrophe while getting ready to go to work on the morning of June 4, 1989. President Mikhail Gorbachev announced the news of a monumental train accident involving several hundred people. Details were very limited, but he was deeply concerned by the number of lives impacted by such a tragedy. The calamity occurred around 1:10 a.m., local Bashkir time. President Gorbachev soon followed his announcement with the additional news that the government had suspended plans to have an inauguration of the new Soviet government and legislature that day. The official celebration of the new National Congress of the People's Deputies would be indefinitely postponed. Gorbachev explained that the citizens of the nation must now stop everything to mourn and honor the hundreds of dead and dying people involved in this terrible event.

The entire Soviet press reported the disaster. Boris Yeltsin personally shared the news with thousands of people attending a rally in Moscow. The political protestors bowed their heads in sorrowful disbelief. Governmental committees for the organization of support and analysis of the accident were established under the guidance of the vice-chairman of the USSR Soviet Ministry, Gennadij Vedernikov. As further details came in, the government reported the truth immediately and in an honest way.

It was touching to see such authentic human responses from government leaders. All the people of Russia were feeling a deep grief and sorrow that only tears could speak. There was a feeling of total and unconditional love. Also, a great deal of love and sympathy immediately started pouring in to the Russian people from around the world.

Upon hearing the news of this terrible accident, I knew I must go to the site immediately. Many people would be in need of support for the mind and emotions as well as the body.

Psychology was my deep passion, and my experience as Dean of the Department of Applied Psychology at the State Open Russian University in Moscow had given me a firm foundation in working with emotions and the mind. As reports started circulating that hundreds of children involved in the accident were being transported to a central location in the nearby city of Ufa, capital of the Bashkir Republic, I called my university and informed them that I would leave the next day to go to Ufa and volunteer my assistance.

I had traveled to Ufa many times to lecture at the Ufa State Educational University. The news would have spread quickly throughout the city. There would be students from the university, many of whom had been in my classes and lectures, who would be able to come to the hospital to help.

Throughout the day, I made personal and professional preparations in order to leave the next morning on the first available flight. Along with the rest of the world, I listened to the news, wanting to learn what had caused such a horrible accident.

As it turned out, June 4 was a monumentally tragic day. News agencies were bombarded with stories of crisis as numerous catastrophic events happened simultaneously, creating worldwide chaos and grief.

In Russia, the announcements about the train tragedy alternated with news of the conflicts in the Uzbek Republic, which were continuing to worsen. Civil unrest had been stirring in Uzbekistan for several weeks, based on ethnic strife that had initially erupted following an argument over the poor quality of some strawberries. On June 4, six thousand soldiers were sent to the area to uphold curfews imposed in the numerous cities where violence and rioting were relentlessly mounting. It was evident that the danger in the area was escalating along with the number of rapidly increasing deaths and hardships.

Announcements of the train disaster also continued, stating that hundreds of passengers had perished in the fires and that it would go on record as one of the world's most tragic rail accidents.

The limited information was interspersed with stories from other countries. News footage from Tehran showed scenes of millions of people who had assembled on June 4 in 90-degree heat to bewail the death of their national leader, the Ayatollah. While these multitudes gathered to pay tribute, eight of the mourners were crushed to death and hundreds of others were injured.

On this same day, the people of the United States of America were anxious because nine of their fellow citizens had been held hostage for several weeks in Iran. A total of fifteen hostages were awaiting the results of immediately pending political negotiations. Now, with the fatal heart attack of the Ayatollah, the negotiations for release took a complicated turn for the worse and were indefinitely suspended. The people of Iran were in mourning, and a new national leader would need to be appointed. The American hostages would have to continue to await their fate.

A brief announcement told about dangerous heavy rains falling in Kegalle, Sri Lanka. Wind and storm clouds had dropped more than eight inches of rain in a record period of time. Because of the inability of the land to absorb the moisture, the outcome of this June 4 storm was a raging flood and mudslide that killed two hundred and fifty people, injuring over one thousand others, and leaving one hundred thousand people homeless.

Continuous pictures and reportage depicting the horrible condition of the train passengers flooded the airways as well as the hearts and minds of the people of Russia. Rumors began to emerge about the possible cause of such a tragedy as authorities continued their search.

The news was again temporarily interrupted to show coverage of military tanks shooting at college students in Beijing's Tiananmen Square. Students had been assembling in this square for two weeks to stage a protest for change. They had been expressing, through song, speeches, and dance, a new vision for the future. Rallying around a collective new thought of political expression, they had camped out together to give voice to their ideas. The military had been outside the Square for the entire two weeks, performing drills and exercises on a daily basis. It was later reported in the Denver Post that "their throaty cadence thundered off the walls of the Great Hall of the People at Mao Tse-tung's mausoleum as they jogged in formation."

At about the same time as the train accident, and also without warning, the military moved in on the collected students in Tiananmen Square. Infantrymen and armored trucks scythed a bloody swathe through hundreds of young men and women. As their voices were brought to silence, the lives of mothers, fathers, sisters, brothers, friends, teachers, and acquaintances were forever changed. The impact of all this simultaneous tragedy was being deeply felt in my country. Had the whole world gone mad?

Finally more news of the trains was broadcast. The cause of the accident was now clear. I will always remember the touching scene on television of Nikolai Ryshkov, chairman of the USSR Soviet Ministry, standing helplessly at the accident site and shedding tears of true compassion. The image of this strong man empathetically weeping served as inspiration to me for weeks.

As the two trains had entered opposite ends of a ravine on their separate tracks, wheel friction had created a spark that ignited liquefied natural gas that had been leaking from thirty-inch pipes nearby. The pipeline carrying liquefied petroleum gas from oilfields in Nizhnevartovsk to refineries in Ufa had ruptured. The leaking fuel contained a mixture of propane, butane, and benzene that partially evaporated, creating a highly combustible formula as it mixed with air.

Photo of the train accident

Rather than investigate a drop in pressure, the operators had turned up the pumps, thus adding to a vast, growing pool of heavy methane vapor that had filled the ravine for three hours prior to the approach of the two trains. The resulting explosion of liquefied gas demolished part of the trans-Siberian railway and killed hundreds of passengers and railroad employees. Many rail cars were crushed and blackened. A shock wave equal to ten thousand tons of TNT threw eleven cars into the air, and twenty-six other cars were burned within ten minutes—seven of them incinerated beyond recognition by the blast of heat that rose to between 1500° and 1800° Fahrenheit. The exploding cloud of gas rose more than 1,600 cubic yards above the earth.

President Gorbachev flew to witness this "major catastrophe." More than 250 acres of trees within a three-mile radius were charred to the ground. Windows were shattered in homes and villages up to seven miles away. Approximately 780 of the 1,284 passengers on the two trains died. Many perished

The remains of trees in a nearby forest

immediately, and others eventually died in hospitals. A total of 383 children were known to be on the trains; however, since tickets were not sold to children under the age of eight, the smallest ones were not initially included in the official count.

At the explosion site, Officer Andrej Doncov was the first to start rescuing the surviving passengers.

An engineer on one of the trains, Victor Bezverchij, was thrown from his locomotive and had his skin burned and some of his limbs broken in the explosion, yet he crawled several kilometers to the nearest village to seek help for the passengers. He reported that, before the explosion, even at his train's high speed, he could smellgas hovering like fog at the level of the train windows.

The driver of the second train, Sergej Stoliarov, along with a co-worker, Marat Ganeev, managed to save more than three hundred people by organizing their immediate rescue from the burning train.

A nearby villager later wrote, "The air itself caught on fire, and the people of the village breathed the flames while they looked at the fire. Many villagers lost their eyesight. Others died from burns in their breathing passages. If we were two kilometers away

Volunteers assisting the rescue

from the epicenter and we were literally deafened by the explosion, then what did the unfortunate train passengers endure?"

One boy lying on a stretcher in an ambulance at the Chelyabinsk airport was so severely injured that a news correspondent simply told the viewers, "He's living."

4. Joining the Team in Ufa

The next day, June 5, I noticed a picture on the news of a young Chinese man standing alone in front of a long row of tanks. He appeared to be demanding that there be a stop to the madness of destruction and chaos. On this day, I was on my way to Ufa to help the children of this disaster face their pain and loss. We too would have to call a halt to the continuing destruction set into motion by our national tragedy.

Aircraft being loaded with supplies

I knew I had to go. I had to do what I could to help them. It was terrible to hear all the stories on television and the radio. Someone had to go help the victims stop their internal chaos. My heart spontaneously reached out to these children, and I felt sure that my knowledge of psychology (the subject I was teaching in Moscow) would be beneficial.

During the entire flight from Moscow, I reviewed strategies and considered various plans for dealing with this crisis situation. Besides teaching psychology, I had previously organized, trained, and assisted with the psychological recovery teams for Chernobyl and the postwar area of Baku. My ideas were based on my training in psychology and on those prior experiences in dealing with catastrophes.

I found myself thinking over and over again about the various ways to organize people, teams, methods, and procedures to deal with this new challenge. Fluent in the concepts and methods of Carl Rogers, Carl Jung, gestalt therapy, psychoanalysis, and art therapy, to name only a few, I assumed that these psychological tools would be all I would need.

I was willing to face the catastrophe head on, confident that my past experience and knowledge would help me do what was needed. Most importantly, I was coming with a pure intention to just be present for these children as they began their journey back to mental health.

I had also packed up my five-year-old son, Denis. He would stay in Ufa with my parents, who were coming there to give help in this way. None of us realized that this was only the beginning of nearly four months of sixteen-hour days.

Ufa, the capital of Bashkortostan, is an industrial city of almost a million people, built near the western Ural Mountains. It was founded in the 16th century by Ivan the Terrible, as a fort from which to fight off nomads. In the 1940s it became active with industries such as oil refining and the manufacture of petrochemicals, processed foods, synthetic rubber, and electrical and mining equipment.

In the early 1980s I had lived in Ufa for several years, and had found it to be a city of excellent universities, offering training in medicine, aviation, mining, and general education. It was here that I had begun my training in pre-medicine, psychology, and foreign languages.

On the day I arrived in Ufa the airport was swarming with people. All flights were being reserved for volunteers coming into the area, while pleasure and business flights had been cancelled. It was a frightening, surreal scene. The sky was filled with helicopters that were to hover like flies for three days solid.

Because of the endless movement of trucks, cars, and helicopters transporting the patients and medical personnel, some of the dazed people who had survived the train accident thought an atomic war had begun. The frenzied presence of air traffic only reinforced this perception.

The majority of the children in the disaster had been brought to a central children's ward for focused care. Those in charge had assigned the children four floors of the building. I came in, explaining that I had a Ph.D. in psychology, and shared my experiences of helping people

Medical personnel preparing transport

in psychological trauma. I offered my assistance freely and emphatically. The organizers were extremely happy to see me because they didn't know how to get so many children and parents out of the state of shock.

The organizers immediately assigned me the task of arranging psychological assistance for the children and their parents. Initially our team consisted of twelve psychologists, but every once in a while I would arrive in the morning to discover that a colleague had returned home. The number of professionals on staff continued to diminish, and by the end of our time with the children only three psychologists had been able to withstand the emotional rigor of working in such an environment.

5. The Thousands Who Came to Help

Help poured in from everywhere. Statistics later documented the scope of the actions of thousands of people who shared their compassion and love in the aftermath of the railway disaster.

Within the first hours following the tragedy:

Volunteer assists with transfusion

🕉 All 938 of the initial survivors of the train wreck were evacuated to nearby hospitals, despite the challenges of reaching them in the ravine where the accident had occurred.

🕉 About 800 people from the Ministry of Internal Affairs came to help, along with 500 soldiers. Also, 3,827 people and 545 vehicles arrived from the Civil Defense Service.

🕉 Hundreds of local citizens donated blood, time, and anything else they could give that would help. Within only the first few hours, 425 liters of blood had been donated.

🕉 Britain's Prime Minister, Margaret Thatcher, sent special waterbeds to support the healing of skin transplants for the burn victims.

🕉 Three dozen restaurants supplied food for the workers. In addition, 4,903 individuals and 269 trucks brought in more food.

Ⓞ For transportation, 550 vehicles and 1,645 buses were brought in.

Ⓞ A thousand railroad tracks were brought in for the reconstruction, as repair work began on the 350 meters of railway that had been destroyed.

Ⓞ Repair work began on the 3,000 meters of electric lines and 1,700 meters of telephone and other communication lines that had been destroyed.

The rescue work that began so immediately was highly organized, calling initially on the skills of fire fighters, military people, and medical personnel. Teams came from all over Russia, and support medical personnel came in from the United States, England, Ireland, Australia, Germany, and Israel.

At the site of the accident, a team of 100 doctors and medical personnel set up tent hospitals in order to provide immediate critical care. Thanks to this service, hundreds of people were later stabilized enough to be moved to nearby hospitals. Among them were 196 children. Depending on the severity of their burns, some patients were sent to Moscow, St. Petersburg, Ufa, and other cities.

Doctors, medical students, medical personnel, and psychologists, as well as countless caring townspeople, worked day and night with the children and adults to support their survival, while the transportation of food and medicine continued around the clock.

The true number of volunteers was beyond calculation. In the first two days, 1,600 people from the army and nearly that many civilians came to offer assistance. Fifteen helicopters from the

Medical personnel returning to the crash site

city of Ufa made 276 flights, airlifting 938 victims and transporting 419 doctors to the site of the accident and to hospitals. Overall, well over 7,000 people came to offer their help.

Free telephone service was set up to handle more than 7,000 calls between cities, and 700 telegrams were sent out. Hundreds of relatives of the people on the trains poured into the area to seek their loved ones. For many of these bereaved family members there was no available infor-

Volunteers worked around the clock to airlift the victims to safety

mation, because the remains of 220 of the passengers were so completely incinerated that they could never be found.

6. AN UNPRECEDENTED SITUATION

Nothing could have prepared me for what I saw when I stepped into the children's ward. As I have described, when I first walked down the corridor, I saw hell. It was like walking into Dante's Inferno. Everyone seemed filled with madness. Children ranging from two to nineteen years of age were screaming, crying, shouting in hysteria, or running about frantically because of their pain and difficulty in breathing. Some were just terribly silent as they sat in deep shock. Several children had no limbs, no fingers, no nose or lips. Many had damaged respiratory systems from the intense heat. All of the children had endured the physical trauma of massive broken bones and burns that covered 40 to 85 percent of their bodies.

The children needed immediate psychological assistance as well as emergency medical assistance. In order to survive, most of these victims had to recover from shock and coma. Due to the extent of their trauma, many of them gave up. During those first few days, one out of every six children died in our arms.

When I first arrived, three of the hospital walls were covered with the names of those who had perished, and each day the list of names grew. Whenever I walked past these walls, my eyes would flood with tears. By the fourth or fifth day, the walls were rapidly being covered with information about children who were in critical states or dying. Passing this area of the hospital became a walk of despair, and I hated the fact that the walls carried only information of death and neardeath.

I had no idea how to work with these children who had no perspective on how to survive. I had been determined to come and help others, yet as I walked through the hospital I realized that everything I had learned was now being turned upside-down. My training had not provided me with any tools to help so many children stuck in the depths of physical and emotional trauma. My prior knowledge was based on cognitive skills, yet these children were unable to access the linguistic level of the brain. They were stuck in the brain stem's flight/freeze response.

I felt stunned by my own lack of tools to help me reach into the inner world of these children. When I saw so many children in coma, in shock, or exhibiting symptoms of deep phobia, I began to feel helpless. I was astonished to realize that none of the methods I had learned in my prior training could be of assistance in bringing these children to the beginning stages of recovery.

Even though I had extensive academic training and professional experience, my knowledge was primarily for people who had already recovered from shock. My professional approaches relied on words, and here before me were a multitude of children who could not even speak. How could I ever reach this many children?

In desperation, and following my own instincts, I picked up a little orange book called *Brain Gym®: Simple Activities for Whole-Brain Learning*, by Dr. Paul E. Dennison and Gail E. Dennison, and opened it.

7. CONSULTING THE LITTLE ORANGE BOOK

In 1988, Dr. Irena Dubroina, scientific director of the Psychological Research Institute of the Russian Academy of Education in Moscow, had invited the neurobiologist Dr. Carla Hannaford to give a presentation on the successful use of Brain Gym. Following her dynamic scientific presentation in Moscow, Dr. Hannaford had thoughtfully left a handful of *Brain Gym®* books as reference for her Russian colleagues.

The "little orange book"
Brain Gym®: Simple Activities for Whole-Brain Learning

Carla Hannaford's research had indeed indicated remarkable results through the use of the Dennisons' movement activities, but it just didn't seem logical that something so simple would have that profound an impact. Due to our lack of understanding of the effectiveness and power of simplicity, most of the books had sat around the institute relatively untouched.

Before I left Moscow to go to the clinic in Ufa, Dr. Natalia Tolstych, director of my psychological research program, suggested that I take along the little orange book, since Dr. Hannaford had reported such remarkable success with the material it contained. For some reason the book did end up in my hands, so I just threw it into my suitcase at the last minute. Upon my eventual return with new respect for the book, Dr.

Tolstych fully supported my idea of undertaking scientific research on the use of the Brain Gym program.

In order to find some way to make a connection with the children in Ufa, I just briefly looked at the pictures in this *Brain Gym®* book. Because these children's injuries were severe, I knew that it would be extremely difficult for them to release the patterns of their emotional pain and corresponding physiological patterns in order to move into the present moment. I decided to begin with three different exercises: Lazy 8s, the Cross Crawl, and Hook-ups.

I approached a child who had been standing and yelling the same sentence for hours, day after day. He cried repeatedly, "We were riding with my grandparents and an explosion happened and my grandmother had fire in her hair."

I looked into the child's frantic eyes, took his hand, and started tracing Lazy 8s. As I did this, with his hand in mine, I repeated his phrases to acknowledge that I had heard his agonized story.

"You were riding with your grandparents and an explosion happened," I said with him, continuing to trace Lazy 8s.

The mutual movement of our hands and arms seemed to stir a sense of surprise and curiosity within the boy. He became distracted from his repetition of hysterical thoughts. I began saying parts of his sentence with him and then broke away from the repeated phrase by adding in other thoughts.

"Yes," I would say, continuing the Lazy 8s, "you were riding with your grandfather and grandmother, and now, look, you are here in this room with me."

He eventually stopped speaking, looked at me, and said, "Yes, now I am here." A nurse standing nearby gave me an understandably grateful look, for she had been hearing the same anguished statement over and over again for hours.

As I turned to see who should receive my attention next, some of the children were running around the ward screaming, "Fire! Fire!" One twelve-year-old boy was lying down, staring off into space, and whispering, "I must go. If I don't, I won't be in time." How I wanted to find a doorway into his mind so I could let him know he was now safe!

I spoke with the children one at a time. With each of them I incorporated the Lazy 8s movement, letting my words honor who they were and the fact that they had experienced the fire. I used movement and words simultaneously, to invite them to step into a new awareness of being present in a reality that was now safe. Time and again I saw how movement was proving to be the means for allowing them to take a step into the present moment, for letting them discover for themselves that they were no longer in danger.

As the children watched or imitated the Brain Gym movements, I continued to explain that I had come to support them and to let them know that they were now in a different time and place that was safe. Even though they were correct about having been in danger in the past, they began to feel that it was safe "here" because "here" rested in the present moment of "now."

Dr. Nikolaj V. Jermoluk (left), chief physician at the Ufa clinic, confers with the nurses

I was always honest with the children. Often people think that if we can forget about a childhood trauma we will "get over it" as an adult. I do not agree. I was learning that it was crucial to accept the children's perception of reality from the past while adding the gift of natural movement. This process invited them to move themselves into the new reality of the present moment. And I found that the Brain Gym movements I was trying out with them allowed the children to experience the past in their own unique way.

I implemented this process with a whole ward of children. I saw that, if I used Lazy 8s with the children, they stopped repeating their mournful statements. The first day, I only used Lazy 8s as I listened, repeating their words and then changing the last half of the sentence, thus inviting the children to shift their focus from their emotional afflictions and bring themselves into the present moment. I would ask questions, such as:

- "What is your favorite color?"
- "I am here to offer help to you, do you understand that?"
- "What is your favorite food?"
- "You are safe now, do you know that?"
- "Do you like to draw?"
- "What did you eat for breakfast?"

Using Lazy 8s seemed to draw the children safely out of being stuck in the survival and protection functions of the brain stem. They were activating and moving into the higher areas of the brain, areas that allowed them to be logical and to see the present reality of being in another time and space.

The next day I introduced the Cross Crawl to a few boys, but only one could copy the movement. Many of the children were unable to move at all due to their burns, so I would demonstrate the activity and just invite them to imagine or pretend they were doing it with me.

I was reminded of the work of the Russian psychologists and researchers V. V. Lebedinsky and S. Y. Rubinstein in the area of child development, and of the discoveries of these two regarding the use of ideomotoric movement to create changes in a person's experience. These respected Russian researchers originally coined the word "ideomotoric," referring to the human ability to create microscopic motor-planning skills, activated in the center of the midbrain, by watching a motion several times. This creates a mental rehearsal that eventually leads to actual movement. This imitation of movement is based on visualization and imagination and is the same sequence that a child carries out in watching and learning the processes of walking and talking. With time, the mental rehearsal becomes reality. Thus, the initial problem that the children's burns prohibited them from physically participating in the movements was overcome by their mentally experiencing the benefits.

Dr. Nikolaj V. Jermoluk, chief physician at the Ufa clinic, liked the results produced by use of the Brain Gym movements because the children were returning to current reality and releasing their fixation on the accident. Momentary relief would come even to children who were still crying and in shock, even if they were able only to watch or imagine these simple movements. In addition to working with the children in the clinic, I was soon called to the emergency ward to assist children and staff members there, so that everyone could learn and use these movements. For many of the children, the Brain Gym movements, along with loving touch and words of encouragement, literally made the difference between life and death.

The children were initially stuck in the brain stem response of protection. Their minds had reacted to the horrors of the accident by freezing in shock or frantically running away from any further perceived danger. I understood that the memory and the shock were so intense that the children had become deeply anchored in a state of hypervigilance and overprotection. Yet everyone now noticed that the use of the Brain Gym movements was creating a new perspective of safety. As I shared these movements, I spoke clearly to each of the children about being a *winner*, about finding the inner courage to triumph despite all the odds.

Next I introduced Hook-ups. It became clear that, as the children began to watch or do this Brain Gym activity, they began to relax. In particular, the element of Hook-ups that involves touching the tongue to the roof of the mouth noticeably helped the children manage their pain. This became an important piece of data. Because large amounts of medication had been needed to control the severity of the children's pain, the doctors were concerned about potential side effects. The medical staff members were relieved to see that less medication was necessary when the children were doing Brain Gym movements.

Dr. Jermoluk (right) confers with a nurse.

The doctors started referring to the movements as "Miracle 8s" and "the Miracle Cross Crawl." Within the first three weeks, they asked me to teach the Brain Gym activities to all the medical students and nursing staff and to the one or two full-time personnel assigned as an aide for each child. Once I had taught the different Brain Gym movements to the entire staff, I asked them to model these movements each time they approached a child's bed. If the children were able to move, they would follow along doing these developmental movements. If they could not move, we found benefit from just having the child imagine doing the movements while they watched the model.

The hospital's medical statistics later showed that, in less than three weeks, the death rate decreased in the wards where the Brain Gym program was implemented. It was further documented that the rate of healing was much faster than in the wards that did not use these movements.

Dr. Svetlana Masgutova & Pamela Curlee

8. "Nikolai, You Are a Winner!"

Because shock can be lethal, it was important to release certain children from their immobile state as soon as possible. I found that children in a state of shock who did the Brain Gym movements were recovering from their shock in two to four days, whereas those who did not do the movements remained in a prolonged state of shock.

One twelve-year-old boy, whom I shall call Nikolai, was always hiding his face and body. He would lie in bed and stare at a wall for days, frozen in fear. So great was his need for isolation, and no therapists had been able to get any response from him.

I said to Nikolai, "If you don't want to look at me, that's okay. I'm here to support you and to let you know that I care about you. My heart is open to you."

Nikolai's self portrait

He started to cry, and told me that it would be better if he were dead.

Thanks to Lazy 8s and the Cross Crawl, Nikolai eventually responded to communication. These activities seemed to add considerably to his feeling of safety. In time, I was able to coax Nikolai to draw. He drew a picture of a face covered with lines, with one eye, no nose, big ears, and fangs at the mouth. He gave me the drawing and told me that it was a picture of himself. All mirrors had been removed from the hospital so that Nikolai and the other children couldn't see how they looked. Nikolai had indeed endured many lacerations, including several facial disfigurations. He explained that the drawing was a picture of himself and that the fangs were symbols of anger, calling the picture "the devil with one eye."

It turned out, however, that Nikolai's depression was caused not only by his injuries, but also by his parents, who when they came to see him were horrified by the thought of their son going back out to face the world. I quickly began to work with the parents. They had put a healthy child on a train, and now that child was dealing with his own shocking physical condition. No wonder the parents required a lot of psychological help and support, as well.

I used art therapy with Nikolai on a daily basis and also had him do the Double Doodle movement from Brain Gym, which quickly became his favorite. As he worked, I told him that he was young and that his skin would heal. We discussed how it doesn't matter what others think; it only matters what we think of ourselves. "You must know that you are very strong," I said. "You have survived against the odds. As a matter of fact, three times, before today, you have proven to me that *you are a winner.*"

I explained these ideas to Nikolai in words similar to the following:

First: In order to come and play on Planet Earth, one must "catch a ride" on a thought. Now, there are actually trillions and trillions of thoughts, and catching the attention of just one takes a lot of wisdom, speed, and courage. Only one very special thought could become the little boy with your name on it. You beat all the odds and connected with that one thought! You were victorious! Only a *winner* could do such a thing.

Second: A race was held, and millions of "racers" were

running to cross the finish line in the greatest marathon of all time. Only one racer could beat the odds and win and have his name announced. And look who won. You won! You were triumphant. You were conceived.

Third: Then, you once again proved that you are a winner when you bravely faced and victoriously found your way through the process called birth. No matter how many times barriers were presented, you met and overcame each obstacle and made your entrance into the world. You had won a third time. And now, here you sit, victorious. You have again triumphed over impossible odds, and you are still here. Do you see, you are a winner again and again! You may be afraid that you will not be accepted in this world, but because you're a winner, maybe it means you have come to teach your parents and others how to have understanding and love in the face of all situations. All I know is that you are a winner, and a winner must teach others how to be the same.

With this invitation to remember his innate wisdom and courage, and from the use of the Brain Gym movements, this young fellow began to move out of his state of shock and depression and find the courage to create a new future.

9. ALLEVIATING PAIN AND FEAR

Soon, because of the rapid improvements in their ability to move and to be present in the moment, more and more children in the ward started drawing. As their desire to communicate became stronger, they asked for paper, paints, crayons, and anything else that they could use to give them the freedom to express their feelings on paper. The first drawings were full of darkness and pain, reflecting the depths of fear and despair that they were experiencing. The most common picture the children drew was of people running with their hair burning. Within seven to ten days, the pictures changed as the children emerged from their emotional and physical shock.

During the first two weeks, most of the children's drawings had to do with fire, explosions, and train crashes. The Calf Pump movement was particularly useful because it helped to release the tendon-guard reflex, which tightens in response to fear. This movement looks similar to the warm-up exercise that runners use. Initially most of the children had to modify the Calf Pump movement in order to do it lying in their beds. Because the lengthening of the calf muscles helps to relax the fight-or-flight reflex, doing this movement helped release feelings of anxiety. Later, when the children could leave their beds, they eagerly continued to do this movement while standing. Through use of the Double Doodle and other homologous movements, they were able to swiftly transition from alarm into purposeful, and eventually playful, movements. Although the stages came step by step, I was astonished by the remarkable speed of the progress.

In the initial stages of his recovery, a young boy whom I shall call Kris drew an abstract picture. He drew the scene of the train accident as if he had viewed it from above the wreckage, showing the center of the explosion and the destruction of the railway.

An aerial view of the accident site   Kris's abstract drawing

This particular boy had been driven to the hospital, not flown in a helicopter (which would have given him opportunity to see the sight he drew). A pilot later commented that the boy's picture was a remarkable representation of the view from above.

Kris's second drawing seemed to be more representative of his own physical experience. It was of a burning horse running in the fire. Kris said he was feeling sad not only for the people who had been killed and injured but also for "the thousands of animals that died." As this thought was distressing to him, I used the Brain Gym movements to help Kris let go of these images.

Many of the children's drawings reflected the same physical trauma that they had themselves experienced. For example, one young girl with widespread burns drew animals in dark brown colors with widely opened eyes. She said this was a picture of bears in a fireball. The bears were frightened and wanted to see the daylight instead of the smoke and darkness of the night.

These bears went to the "forest hospital," where other animals tried to help them, but the child initially insisted that they were still afraid of fire.

Naturally the children had a fire phobia. The sight of a worker lighting a cigarette would easily trigger this phobia, and some of the children would run off screaming. I had the children sit or stand in the Hook-ups position or just imagine doing this simple Brain Gym activity. Through the use of this Hookups posture, the phobias began to be released.

A child's picture of bears in a fireball

Over time, the children drew the fire in their pictures smaller and smaller. And as they discussed new ways of looking at the fire, the children would move with Lazy 8s, the Cross Crawl, Hook-ups, or the Calf Pump. When they felt safe to look at fire in a new way, we would draw pictures showing constructive uses of fire. While doing a Brain Gym movement like Hookups, we imagined sitting around a fire with friends and singing songs about being a *winner*. At the end we would all do the Cross Crawl. The children's desire for survival was being drawn out of them through the use of art, Brain Gym movements, and psychotherapy.

Because the explosion had happened at night, other common fears among the children were those of death and darkness. Also, many of the children were afraid of any kind of train or transport.

I offered the children therapy for all of their senses. They had to relearn that it was safe to see, touch, taste, smell, and hear. Because their orientation to the sense of smell was fixated on burning skin, bones, and metal, the slightest scents were often irritating. The children needed to have their sensory channels experience a reeducation in pleasant associations. This idiosensory work was done by letting them experience contrasting tastes and smells. We explored the contrasts of chocolate, lemon, ice cream, salt, and spices, because nothing was tasty to the children at first. Before playing with their memories of the differences between sweet-spicy or sweet-pungent smells, we did Brain Gym activities to create a sense of safety.

Our work continued with all of the fears: the fear of fire, of burning people, and of dead people, trains, burn therapy, and treatments. I was again astonished at the rapid rate of improvement that occurred daily, and I decided to incorporate Brain Gym movements into every one of my psychotherapy sessions. Later I was able to make a correlation between the Brain Gym movements and natural developmental reflexes, and to understand why the effects were so profound.

Being a scientist, I promised myself that I would set up in-depth studies of the phenomena resulting from these exercises because I knew of nothing else that could take children so quickly from a past tragedy into present reality. Not only did I eventually get Russian universities and scientists to study why Brain Gym works so well, but I later also had occasion to experience the material first-hand when my personal life was struck by tragedy and loss. Using all of the skills that the children had co-created with me, I later moved beyond the murder of my beloved twenty-year-old sister, Helen, and eventually rediscovered and even deepened my sense of reverence and joy for the gift of life.

10. Miracles Happen

The in-service session I held to teach all the medical students and personnel how and when to do the Brain Gym movements was gratifying. I always find it rewarding to work with colleagues who are open-minded. The medical staff's understanding of the importance of implementing this unique physiological assistance created the space for the children's emotional, mental, and physical survival. Most of the staff members were grateful for the breakthrough discovery that movement can result in growth and significant change in traumatized children. On the other hand, it was frustrating to interact with those few colleagues who closed their minds and refused to see the value of the new work being offered.

I had worked for three weeks with a nine-year-old boy I shall call Mikhail, who had lost both of his parents in the disaster. Because of the benefits Mikhail had received from doing the Brain Gym movements, over time the doctors were giving him less and less medication. He was beginning to walk again, and was showing signs of remarkable progress.

Then one day, without warning, Mikhail suddenly began to scream as he tore clothing off of his aide and himself. A psychiatrist immediately came and gave him medication. Earlier in the day, Mikhail had become hysterical and aggressive after being asked by his aide to clean up some juice he had spilled. The staff called me, and I immediately began to do some Brain Gym activities with Mikhail. In all, I worked with him three times during a four-hour period. The boy was angry, and kept repeating that he wanted to die. We later learned that he had received a phone call to inform him that his grandmother had died. No one had prepared him for this shocking information, and Mikhail was devastated, thinking that he was now to be an orphan for the rest of his life.

Mikhail and I kept doing Lazy 8s and other Brain Gym movements together as we talked. I explained to him that he was brave to have attempted to handle such information by himself, adding that we had many strong people working at the clinic who were there to assist him with such situations. While sitting in Hook-ups, he began to tell his story of what had happened to his grandmother. I acknowledged his grief as we continued doing various Brain Gym movements, until he calmed down and seemed to have rediscovered a feeling of safety within himself.

In just one evening, that child returned to a balanced sense of reality and was ready to move forward again. I wrote a note in his chart, explaining that Mikhail was now psychologically okay and would not need further medicating drugs. But when I returned the next morning, Mikhail was in a state of stupor from heavy medication. Having seen other children suffering and even dying from the side effects of medications, and because I had clearly stated that drugs were no longer needed for this child, I confronted the psychiatrist and shouted to him that he must never touch these children again. The man never returned to my floor.

My anger and frustration stemmed from the fact that, every day, survival required a great effort for so many of those children. One tenyear-old boy and his sister had struggled to endure for twenty days. Because of the amount of medication the boy had needed to control his pain, his kidneys were beginning to shut down, and the doctors were concerned that his prognosis did not look good. His physiological state worsened, and he ended up in the emergency room with kidney failure. In response to one doctor's request, I then worked frequently with this ten-year-old. Every day we would do the Cross Crawl, Positive Points, the Thinking Cap, and Lazy 8s, as I told him stories about a brave boy who kept thinking "I will survive because I remember what it feels like to be a *winner*."

"You are a winner," I would tell him, "and you have only one choice, and that one choice is to find many other positive choices." I am happy to report that this boy did manage to survive.

Other children in the emergency room were also reaching critical states, and the doctors said they would not survive. Some were in a coma and others were screaming for drugs to ease their pain. Many struggled with breathing. Sharing Brain Gym with them seemed to foster their ability to breathe and relax. The sensation of touch on the unburned parts of their bodies became very important in their recovery. The children were crying out to receive the gift of touch. Over and over, I told them how strong they were, while modifying the Brain Gym movements to fit each child's needs and movement abilities. We had all become one big family—working together, moving together, and surviving together. Miracles happened. Six children in the emergency room, whom the doctors had said could never survive, did survive.

11. TWO-HANDED RAINBOWS

I believe that nature has programmed us to survive, and that the power of natural survival methods can be used to awaken hope in people who are under stress. In Ufa, I discovered that adding developmental movements speeds up and enriches the process of remediation. For example, homologous movements (such as Brain Gym's Double Doodle) improve physical and emotional coordination. Children naturally clap their hands out of joy. When in fear, they shake both hands wildly in the air. These separate yet simultaneous and symmetrical hand movements allow the activity of the brain to move out of the brain stem and go into the cortex. Each hemisphere is able to reestablish links of communication within itself, preparing for action. Brain activity begins to move independently and yet simultaneously within the left and right hemispheres, and this serves as a foundation for future integrated communication in the cortex. Only then can we be ready to interpret trauma fully and objectively.

I used the wisdom of natural body movement to give the children a new perspective from which to recall the fires. Homologous movements were exceptionally useful in helping them to move from the memories of the past to the current reality of "now."

The children used these movements to release their fear of fire by pretending to stomp on a fire with both feet or pound it out with both hands. The experience of clapping both hands to smother the fire also allowed the children to revisit the strength of homologous movement.

For the same reason, I had the children draw all their

pictures of fire with two hands at the same time, making use of the Double Doodle activity. For the children, expressing their thoughts and feelings as they drew created a bridge between the past and the present moment. While moving in this way, they told imaginary stories with anger, then with a seriousness, and then with laughter. (While they were getting in touch with their anger, no shouting or screaming was permitted, because these sounds had been expressed in the early days and would only take them back to the past.)

The children drew every day with both hands simultaneously, or if they had only one hand, they would draw with that single hand, imagining it was "made of two hands." If they drew portraits of favorite people, they were encouraged to stay away from thoughts of loved ones who had died in the crash. Dealing with these memories could only come later, when they could view these truths from a place of inner safety.

These young patients loved homologous movements and referred to them as the "rainbow journey." They created rainbows in the air, first starting with their two hands above them and meeting in the center; then they would move their hands in opposite directions, creating an arch. Some children had to imagine this movement, since they could not move due to the severity of their burns. Repeating this activity over and over, they imagined and talked about different colors of the rainbow. I would suggest the color red, which the children associated with fire, last of all, and only if the children seemed ready to handle it. All the other colors were used to bring safety to the color red.

The children often repeated the rainbow movements at different speeds and with various colors and sounds, as well as with stories about strength and wisdom and being a *winner*. Often, when I would walk into a room to work with a group of children, I would find them telling one another rainbow stories and creating the rainbows in the best form that they could. They

Dr. Svetlana Masgutova & Pamela Curlee

seemed to instinctively know that this basic developmental movement was a key to their recovery, because they made repeated, spontaneous use of the movements.

They formed the rainbows with both hands moving outward from the middle; then they would move from the outside and come back to the middle. Instead of being stuck in an extended mode of protection and guard, they would shift their peripheral vision to the experience of relaxed centralization. If one has suffered a trauma, the peripheral vision may become set in hypervigilance as a form of protection. When the visual system is overused in this way by perpetual defense, it becomes exhausted and ineffective. Creating the rainbow with both hands in a playful way allows the eyes to finally release this overprotective posture, creating a more relaxed and centralized visual acuity. In the instance of the children in Ufa, this relaxed visual state would later help them improve their reading skills when they returned to school.

Our work with movement also allowed the children to develop an expanded sense of where they were in time and space. They would move with both hands while they were standing, sitting, and lying down. These movements were physically preparing them to be able to explore different levels of balance and stability with a sense of safety and play. Eventually they would "walk" across the rainbows and tell stories to one another, which allowed them to move into more advanced developmental movements of a cross-lateral nature. Some would cross-crawl over the rainbow, telling funny stories as they moved. I then presented combinations of movements, offering new challenges to some and comic relief to others as I made "silly mistakes." Doing the Cross Crawl with a variety of songs brought both challenge and laughter. Some children actually regained their ability to laugh within five days, while others took a month to rediscover it. Often laughter became a relief valve through which crying and screaming could follow.

The Lazy 8s movement also created rapid self-education of the mind and body. The children's eyes relearned to feel safe looking in all directions. Later, the children used Alphabet 8s when writing. They started by practicing individual letters in the Lazy 8s on their paper, and then they would write a message like "I love myself" while using this Brain Gym movement. They became so excited about this achievement that they would follow this exercise by giving themselves a hug. Eventually they used the same process to write each letter of their message sentences, saying, "I am a *winner*" or "I am strong/ healing/recovering/developing."

12. REGAINING SELF-WORTH

I found it important to understand and accept the stages of grief without making shallow promises. The children were teaching themselves, through movement, that they were *winners*. Experience must come first, and encoding the experience with words ideally comes second. Otherwise the words are empty and hollow, and carry only the meaning perceived by the person speaking. When the experience naturally draws out the words from within, the meaning is deep and authentic.

I followed the needs of the children by using empathetic listening skills that allowed me to hear, be congruent, and share open and honest feelings from both sides, while doing the Brain Gym movements. The important thing was to feel the feelings, follow the children's emotional experience step by step, and combine this exploration with the Brain Gym activities.

Once the sense of survival was experienced and then stabilized by the children, we began preparation for their future, exploring selfimage, self-value, and self-worth. The children learned that they must be ready to teach others that they were winners for yet a fourth time, because they had gained strength through their victories. I encouraged them to go out and teach others about this wisdom. The children would have to learn to notice their own behaviors of manipulation and compensation that could put them back in the victim role, thereby causing them to cry out for attention and protection again. They had experienced what it was like to move out of the need for protection and into the place of development. They would have to be ready to explain this to the friends, teachers, parents, and neighbors who might offer them overprotection or go into survival reactions themselves when confronted with these children.

Most of the children had gone through a phase of hating their damaged bodies and faces. I often shared fairy tales, metaphors, and stories with high moral values, in order to invite them to experience a perspective of self-respect. The following story is one I told to one girl who spoke of her concern about the reactions of others regarding her face:

A young woman and a young man were falling in love. The girl's face was not very pretty, so she didn't believe her sweetheart when he said he loved her. She felt it was impossible for anyone to truly love her because of the way she looked. The two of them had become very good friends, and yet she continued to feel bad about herself. One day she decided to leave the city and find someone who could change her face. She lived in a remote village in the mountains of Russia, but she had heard of a man who had some herbs that could possibly change her looks. She found the man and put on a mask of herbs, waiting to become beautiful. When she returned with the mask on, the boy was frantically running around looking for the girl he loved. As she stood in front of him, he cried because he had lost his best friend and could find her nowhere. The next day she decided to remove the mask and return to him as she was. He saw her and took her into his arms with joy! The face didn't matter. It was the person inside that he loved, and now she understood the true meaning of beauty.

Before leaving the hospital, the girl with the ravaged face came up to me and said, "I am the happiest person in the world, and I am the strongest, as well, because I have survived. I am a *winner* inside, and I know how to take the *winner* into my future."

13. Natural Developmental Movements

It is the instinct to move that first motivates an infant to explore various stages and transitional phases of mobility. This allows for natural growth and development. When a block is thrown into the path of life, it becomes useful to return to the original, internal wisdom of movement in order to build a new life. In the life of an infant, or of a person suffering from posttraumatic stress disorder, reconstructing developmental movements crucially influences the brain in its mental, emotional, and intellectual processes. To quote Brain Gym cooriginator, Dr. Paul E. Dennison, "Movement is the door to learning." This is a basic premise of life.

Developmental movements such as the Brain Gym activities remind the body of its primary strategies, all based on the security of survival. Examples of primary strategies include body centering and straightening as well as homologous, homolateral, and crosslateral movements. The Brain Gym learning program supports these natural strategies, because its movements and exercises remind us that we are safe and secure, thus allowing us to incorporation the new information so crucial to our physical development and emotional growth.

These natural developmental movements actually allow people of any age to access their own inner resources and wisdom so that they can literally and metaphorically draw out from within them their own growth and development. Further, these natural movements provide motivation for recovery because they reactivate the primary experience of sensory and motor integration. This state of physical integration creates a foundation of safety upon which learning can then take place.

Examples of art work after using *Brain Gym® Movements*

Five-year-old girl: Traumatic images (on top of the picture) shows survival from the catastrophe. Later a path brings the child to her happy home after the accident.

Five-year-old-girl: Drawing of animals, flowers, and even insects that survived the incident.

Six-year-old girl: "I survived".

Six-year-old girl: Picture made using Lazy 8s.

Dr. Svetlana Masgutova & Pamela Curlee

Six-year-old girl: Picture made using Lazy 8s.

Examples of *Brain Gym*® Activities

Lazy 8s

A Lazy 8 is drawn on its side and includes a definite midpoint and separate left and right visual fields, joined by a continuous line. Begin by placing your thumb directly on your visual midline, straight in front of your face. Draw a circle up and to the left, returning to the midline position. Continue with a smooth movement up and to the right, drawing a second complete circle. Lazy 8s are similar to the infinity symbol used in physics. They enable us to cross the visual midline without interruption, thus activating both the left and the right eye and integrating the left and right visual fields.

The Double Doodle

Begin by creating a free-form "scribble" with both hands. Now draw with both hands mirroring each other: "in," "out," "up," and "down." Draw different shapes, patterns, or pictures with both hands at the same time. The Double Doodle is a bilateral drawing activity which is done on the midline to establish direction and orientation in space relative to the body. The movement develops centralization in the visual midfield, as well as left and right discrimination.

Dr. Svetlana Masgutova & Pamela Curlee

The Cross Crawl

In this contralateral exercise, similar to walking in place, alternately move one arm and its opposite leg and then the other arm and its opposite leg. Because the Cross Crawl accesses both brain hemispheres simultaneously, this is an ideal warm-up for all skills that require crossing the body's lateral midline. This activity improves right/left coordination, and activates the brain for enriched visual, auditory, and kinesthetic skills.

The Thinking Cap

Use thumbs and index fingers to pull the ears gently back and "unroll them." Begin at the top of the ear and gently massage down and around the curve, ending with the bottom lobe. This can be repeated three or more times. This Brain Gym activity improves head turning, enhancing listening and the auditory skills of attention, discrimination, and memory.

Hook-ups, Part One

Cross the ankles. Next, extend your arms out in front of you, thumbs down and backs of the hands touching. Now cross one wrist over the other, touching palms together. Interlace your fingers and draw your hands in toward the chest. Sit (or stand) this way for one minute, breathing deeply, with your eyes closed and your tongue on the roof of your mouth.

Hook-ups, Part Two

During Part Two of Hook-ups, uncross your legs and put your fingertips together, continuing to breathe deeply for another minute. This Brain Gym activity gives rise to a sense of balance, grounding, and emotional centering. Note: The five Brain Gym activities described here, as well as the other Brain Gym movements mentioned in this book, are from Brain Gym®: Teacher's Edition, ©1989 and 1994 by Dennison and Dennison and published by E d u–K i n e s t h e t i c s, Inc, www.BrainGym.com

Dr. Svetlana Masgutova & Pamela Curlee

14. A Resource for Happiness

The strength of the *winner* within is the source of survival and a resource for being happy in any physical, intellectual, or emotional state. The human response to a trauma is characterized by four basic stages: (1) protection for survival (freeze or flight), (2) reaction for survival (fight or flight), (3) growth (stopping to think and learn), and (4) development (implementation and modeling of the new learning).

Accessing the wisdom of primary and natural movements in the body supports the completion of all four of these stages. Inviting both the physical and the emotional strength of nature to awaken within creates a space where it is safe to let go of any repetitive story of mistakes, failures, and blame.

The children I knew in Ufa met the challenge, gathered their natural internal resources, and moved through the entire experience of survival. The catastrophe taught them that they were heroes. They were brave and strong ones who fought emotional and physical battles against all odds until, eventually, they brought themselves successfully into the new reality and life in front of them. They met fear face to face, released it, and replaced it with the wisdom of the winner inside. From this place of wisdom, the children prepared themselves and others for a new future. Like the boy in Tiananmen Square, they created a picture of courage to show to the world. They also bravely stood in the face of fear and demanded that it stop.

You did so well, my children. When faced with the many options of perception, you chose to reveal the deepest truths. Yes, you stood face-to-face with the fears connected to catastrophe. And, yes, the tragedy you lived through altered the world you once knew. How easy it would have been for you to choose to continue running away or hiding from this fearful event!

Yet you chose to move into an inner place of simple truth. From the depth of the winner within you, you created a manifestation of the real "you." Your self-discovery was based on the experience of facing endless challenges, big and small. Your bravery, wisdom, strength, and inner knowing, which allowed you to overcome countless daily obstacles, remained present to assist you through the aftermath of the catastrophe. You showed us all how purposeful movement and touch can simply reconnect us with inner intelligence, which allows us to move forward. We thank you for reminding us of the natural wisdom within the body. Your extraordinary story will long continue to serve as an inspiration to us all.

THE EPILOGUE

After I returned to Moscow, I initiated extensive research into why the Brain Gym movements could produce such profound results. The little orange book, *Brain Gym®: Simple Activities for Whole-Brain Learning* by Dr. Paul Dennison and Gail Dennison, had sat in my office for almost a year prior to the Ural Mountain tragedy. I had opened the book with skepticism, only to place it back on the shelf. I just couldn't understand how using the Brain Gym activities could have any major effect. And yet, when the information was used in Ufa, I saw that it had a deep and lasting impact, just as Dr. Hannaford had reported.

Could something so simple have such truly profound effects? My experiences with those children hovering between life and death had answered my question. The implementation of the Brain Gym activities had brought remarkable and significant results, and those activities deserved research and investigation.

Once back in Moscow, I shared my findings with many of my colleagues, and the research began. Since 1989, the following programs and research projects have been created:

Ⓞ Research work with innovative kindergarten and elementary grade classes, in which the goal was to determine the effects of movement on the motor, emotional, and intellectual development of children between the ages of three and ten. Brain Gym activities and balance procedures were added to the children's daily routines, and the research results documented the Brain Gym program's unique and remarkable support of natural learning.

🕉 Further research on the Educational Kinesiology learning program was conducted in the Laboratory of Personal Development, part of the Russian Educational Academy in Moscow.

🕉 Still further research was done by Vera Sirotkina and myself, based on galvanic skin response (a change in the ability of the skin to conduct electricity, caused by an emotional stimulus such as fright). The study showed why the Brain Gym movements could produce such positive results. Research was also done to find frequencies of music that correlate with the profound effects of the four basic movements used in a preparatory Brain Gym procedure known as PACE™.

🕉 Correlations were drawn between the experiences in Ufa and the work of Russian developmental psychologist Lev Vygotsky, creator of a theory regarding the interaction of natural and social development. Vygotsky presented his concepts regarding reflexes between 1930 and 1934. He taught that reflexes do not disappear; in fact, he found that primitive reflexes become integrated into higher levels of brain structures and become the basis of more mature levels of movement. Rather than becoming extinguished, the reflexes serve as a foundation of growth and are available later if needed in emergency situations. Vygotsky also taught that the reflexes are for protection and development.

🕉 Further correlations were drawn between the experiences in Ufa and Vygotsy's work regarding the idea of natural crisis being a foundation for learning:

Phase One: One becomes stuck in the experience of a crisis.

Phase Two: The experience of the crisis opens up an "aha" state because the individual finds another pattern to use as a basis for development. The crisis then becomes a foundation for higher levels of learning.

Ⓞ Correlations were also drawn between the experiences in Ufa and the work of Dr. Nikolai Bernstein, the Russian physiologist who documented that muscles and movement can become stuck in inefficient patterns, both conscious and unconscious. He demonstrated the neurological link between reflexes and movement patterns of survival. This information formed part of the basis of extensive coursework now offered on the study and integration of reflexes, taught by my staff and myself.

Ⓞ In Russia, mobile Brain Gym centers were established within seven time zones to bring the knowledge of the Brain Gym program to thousands of people.

Ⓞ My research based on 2,400 participants inspired an article entitled, "The Cross Crawl and Lazy 8s: Diagnostic Possibilities and Developmental Effects." This work detailed research in innovative kindergarten and elementary-grade classes in more than forty Russian cities.

Ⓞ I have published more than seventy other articles in Russia and Poland on the developmental effects of the Brain Gym activities and the benefits of reflex-integration programs.

Ⓞ More than ten thousand drawings of Lazy 8s have been collected in Russia for analysis of learning styles and verification of development.

Ⓞ The fields of Developmental Neuro Kinesiology and the Masgutova Method™ have been created, based on findings of the profound benefits of awakening and integrating the dynamic and postural infant and lifelong reflexes.

Ⓞ Masgutova Tactile Integration has also been created based on the initial benefits experienced by the children of Ufa. In this technique, touch and movement are found to be crucial to learning and survival.

☺ Ongoing research has been established in coordination with Dr. O. Fred Donaldson, a pioneer in the field of Original Play (and the creator of that term), to show the profound and lasting benefits of integrating the gift of natural play to enhance the development of physical, emotional, mental, and social skills.

☺ The International Dr. Svetlana Masgutova Institute™ in Poland has been established (www.masgutovainstitute.com or www.MasgutovaMethod.com). Here, I invite all participants to rise to the peak of their physical, mental, and emotional potential by experiencing Brain Gym, Masgutova Tactile Integration, Psych Kinesiology, and Art Kinesiology™.

☺ My manual for the Art Kinesiology class has been approved by the Art Education Scientific Research Institute of the Russian Educational Academy.

☺ Plans are currently under way to create a university program in the United States that will share the technologies of the Masgutova Method™: Masgutova Tactile Integration, Brain Gym®, Art Kinesiology™, Proprioception Therapy, and Psych Kinesiology. This university is to be founded on the idea of establishing an educational program based on active technology to bring natural recovery and true integration to people's mental, physical, and emotional needs. This technology will serve as a foundation or basis for learning with ease. For information regarding this developing program, refer to www.masgutovamethod.com.

☺ The International Dr. Svetlana Masgutova Institute™ in Poland and the Svetlana Masgutova Educational Institute in U.S. has established a world-renowned camp/conference to which therapists, parents, and clients come from all over the world to learn and experience this new technology of

Neuro-Sensory-Motor and Reflex Integration, as well as the integration of dynamic and postural reflexes. At the camp/conference, remarkable progress is seen is seen for those with learning challenges, intellectual delay, ADD, and ADHD. This progress is matched by participants' equal success in moving beyond previous limitations in the areas of autism, cerebral palsy, and developmental delays and post traumatic stress syndrome.

16. THE THEORY BEHIND THE INTERVENTIONS AT UFA

As one begins to explore the language of the body, it becomes clear that we humans assume different physiological postures as part of our natural survival-instinct response. We experience these physiological reactions as emotions that we can eventually identify as fear, anger, rage, apathy, frustration, anxiety, hopelessness, and so on.

In response to our feeling overwhelmed by danger, the body's genius (a gift from our DNA) automatically puts us into various stages of fight/flight/freeze behavior to help us through the moment of trauma. These reactions are based on an innate wisdom that allows us to respond appropriately to any threat to our safety. These inborn strategies activated in the body for protection and survival are safely stored in the cells of our physiology. Without this collection of genetic wisdom triggered through experience, the body wouldn't know what to do when faced with danger.

A response of this kind is known as a reflex, a complex of reactions of the body-mind system in response to external and internal stimuli. Reflexes are not just there arbitrarily; they actually exist in the context of a whole picture called development. In the 1930s, developmental psychologist Lev Vygotsky challenged the concept that reflexes become inhibited. His questioning of the repression of reflexes was based on his observation that reflexes come back on line to serve us during times of stress, emergency, accidents, and emotional breakdown. In these situations they often help us to survive. Therefore,

Vygotsky asserted, we must do everything we can to fully develop the reflexes and reintegrate them with higher brain functioning. His view was that primary movements and reflexes never disappear. Following trauma, Vygotsky said we must reintegrate these reflexes so that we can act from love rather than from fear.

Automatic movements and postures are designed to protect us when survival is challenged and our reflexes ideally inform us about possible danger and organize our protection processes. They are naturally activated and then, ideally, once the danger has passed, their function is released and reintegrated. However, time is a construct of what Dr. Paul Dennison refers to as the logic brain. So, to the rest of the brain and body, moments of trauma might seem timelessly present. Often the brain and body remain fearful that a traumatic experience may recur without warning. The motto "Be prepared" becomes "Remain in a constant state of reaction and fear."

We also tend to retain these reflex responses as reactions to anything that reminds us of past traumatic events. Old memories or a new shock can stimulate the areas of the brain that freeze us in a physiological experience of fear. We then come to believe that it is safer to live in a state of perpetual defense, "just in case the danger comes back," and this keeps our survival reflexes in constant use.

Shock is the normal physiological effect when the protection and survival responses become prolonged and chronically stuck. This leads to a hypervigilant state of physical and emotional protection in which it seems the only way to survive is to freeze or to move frantically and without purpose. In such a state of continual reactivity, the lower areas of the brain have purposely taken charge for safety from real or perceived danger. Thus, words and reasoning, the province of the higher levels of the brain, have little or no effect during an initial state of shock. Logic is not yet an option, because the mind and physiology are permanently employed in preparing for the danger that seems perpetually present.

A perpetuated and exhausted reflex can never work as effectively as a matured and integrated reflex. Paradoxically, our ability to feel safe is actually diminished when our reflexes for protection and survival have to work twenty-four hours a day, seven days a week. The overuse of the physiological mechanisms for survival create an illusion of security, yet the body actually remains in a state of stress and tension and is therefore is only capable of hiding, fighting, or running. Then the physiological mechanisms are too overextended to be able to serve in a time of real need. Additionally, an unintegrated reflex also distracts the attention of the mind-body system and blocks rational and reasoning processes in the higher parts of the brain.

The freeze reaction literally stops the movement of the body in order to allow us to "hide" for a moment. As external physical movements slow down, the cognitive skills can speed up. This natural physiological reaction creates an illusion of shelter for thinking and planning, based on a sense that invisibility is creating momentary safety. Even though the body is motionless, the perceptual system is on full-time guard. The senses of seeing, hearing, and feeling are extremely heightened and reactive in an attempt to find a way out of danger. However, adrenaline and cortisol increase dramatically, inhibiting the frontal lobe function. Therefore, the ability to actually access clear cognition and reasoning is blocked. Instead of finding real solutions, the brain remains stuck in reaction or depression.

When a physical shock prolongs this natural impulse to freeze, a vicious circle is created. The main task is then to restart movement, and the most effective circuit breaker of physical shock is developmental movement. Touch is also an essential factor in the reawakening of the nervous system and movement. These are exactly the same principles that an infant follows for the stimulation of growth and development.

Emotional shock creates a negative conceptual cycle. In a desperate search for logic and explanation, one's thinking becomes dominated by the memorization and dramatic replay of the traumatic situation. It is experienced, expressed, and anchored in the story and history of the shock, horror, and terror. When this survival strategy is prolonged beyond the time of actual danger, the mind and body can become anchored in a negative cycle comparable to that of a broken record. While all fearful thinking is based on this constant repetition of negative events, the physiological response can become correspondingly stuck in the fight/flight/freeze reflexes. This is experienced as different degrees of hysteria or depression.

Because the children who survived the train wreck felt as if disaster would strike repeatedly, they remained stuck in their patterns of fight/flight/freeze. I knew I had to help them release themselves from these patterns in order to begin the process of change. Otherwise, revisiting the experience of the fire with their protection and survival mechanisms still activated would only cause these children to dig deeper into their protective strategies.

If one continues to live with the freeze/flight or fight/flight reaction in perpetual activation, the experience of being over-whelmed or of trying too hard will also continue, because the map of this behavior is firmly held within the body. As long as the body believes the danger is still there, it must, by natural law, protect itself. The conscious mind may come up with another idea, yet the body will remain stuck in the original story. And the ruts only get deeper. For as long as the mind and the body are not in agreement on which story to believe, the old physiological perception of danger will continue and little change will be noticed in behavior or in repetitive mental stories. On the other hand, when the body is able to change and feel safe, it is natural for the state of mind to change, as well.

The feeling of authentic safety is possible only when we can release the biological memory of the need for protection and survival. Remaining in a frozen state of perpetual protection leads only to exhaustion of the system and forces one to live with merely the illusion of safety. Anatomically, protection and survival functions are located in the brain stem and limbic area. When one can function from higher cortex levels of the brain and, therefore, actually feel safe, the lower levels of the brain no longer need to remain in a state of reaction. Slow, integrative cross-lateral movements activate these higher centers of the brain, and thereby create a natural transition into higher brain functioning. Movement activates the motor cortex in the frontal lobes, which leads to high-level reasoning, creativity, and connection with the emotions of altruism, love, empathy, and compassion. One is then ready to move forward with an integrated mind and physiology.

The primary means of communication between the brain and the rest of the body is movement and touch. The children in Ufa naturally responded to the invitation to movement because it was the only language they could access. Movement created inner stability for them. They would beg for touch wherever they were not burned because, again, touch was a language of connection that literally allowed them to stay in touch. The children also found that the holding of specific points on their feet brought them relief. (I have continued the study of these points and have mapped them under the name of sensori-motor and neuro-motor points). Every time such a specific means of touch was used, it sent a message to the brain to release the state of perpetual tendon-guard reflex. It was also noted that the moro and the fear of paralysis reflexes would relax, and the child would feel safer. Touch also sent a message that the child was not isolated because there was someone there who could help them get back "in touch" with current reality. Because of these gifts of movement and touch, the children were later able to regain access to their creativity, analytical thinking, and verbal language.

Those brave children helped teach me that necessary physiological shifts come quickly and naturally through Brain Gym and other developmental movements. One main reason that movement is so effective is because it is the natural language of the body and the key to releasing, maturing, and reintegrating primitive and lifelong reflexes. In the field of psychology, four stages of response to trauma have been established:

1. Protection for survival (freeze or flight)

2. Reaction for survival (fight or flight)

3. Growth (stopping to think and learn)

4. Development (implementation and modeling of the new learning)

The third and fourth stages, growth and development, require a release of the physiological posture of the first two stages. Reaction can then become "pro-action."

Once the reflex patterns have been reintegrated through developmental movement, the body and mind have a new foundation for the growth and development stages. Physical and mental skills and abilities, along with new levels of coordination, naturally emerge during these stages. One now becomes able to construct new ways of looking at old experiences. Because the body experiences a state of integration and safety, the mind quickly and naturally begins to experience freedom, creativity, and healthy perspectives.

In order to access this place of growth and development, we are learning to reverse the traditional approach in an interesting way. Instead of changing the mind in order to change how one feels about an experience, we address the physical feeling and the physiological response, and thereby find that the mental interpretation shifts as a by-product, not as the goal. This is the gift of natural developmental movement.

This knowledge and process invites us to expand beyond the old process-and-result orientation. According to the Polish scientist Alfred Korzybski, "The map is not the territory." By this he meant that we can actually be limited by the knowledge we hold within the structures of our language and our nervous system. The map of experiences recorded in the mind and body is not the true current territory. When words and reactions from the past have become stamped in our field of perception, we are at risk of having them govern all our future thoughts and feelings for the continued sake of survival.

Our true potential is based on releasing these mental and physical patterns so that growth and development are acknowledged with ease, comfort, playfulness, and joy. When the body is at home in a field of all possibilities (the true territory), the mind is comfortable in exploring the map of the past and in becoming creative for the future. "Now" has expanded to comfortably hold "all."

17. MOVING BEYOND SURVIVAL

Facilitating the children in moving away from the horror of the past and into the present moment was our challenge, and for this the natural movements of the Brain Gym program seemed to offer the necessary bridge. Once the children could experience being in the here and now, they could feel the safety of the present moment. They could then begin to process the catastrophe they had survived and release their need for continual protection. Then they would be free to begin moving into the stages of growth and development.

By looking at the overall picture of their survival strategies, I could see that the children had initially chosen to stay in protection and reaction. For example, Nikolai, whose body and mind had endured such unspeakable trauma, found that the only way to continue surviving was to stay in the freeze/protection stage by lying on his bed and staring at the wall for days. Even though he didn't move physically, his mind and perceptual systems were working overtime. Taking in all the sights and sounds was possible for him only because he remained very still. Believing himself to be invisible, he could maintain the illusion of being safe from future attack. For him to move and think at the same time remained impossible. However, by staying in this response for such a long period, he had days to recall—and therefore memorize—his traumatic experience. His frozen state eventually turned to depression and the desire to end his life. By the time I was able to start working with him, Nikolai had nearly lost all hope.

Mikhail's response, on the other hand, was initially one of

hysteria—the extreme emotional experience of being unable to stop and think. Thinking, for Mikhail, could only happen when he was moving. In such a severe case as his, the search for the ability to think was accompanied by screaming, yelling, crying, running, walking, and frantic movement. All these responses were the attempts of the body-mind system to survive.

A deep shock response of self-protection involves both the emotions and thinking. This response was quite strong for most of the children for the first few hours or days, and I knew it was important to invite them to come out of this state as soon as possible. My work provided clear evidence that, without movement, the state of shock was prolonged. Yet, with the addition of purposeful movement, like Brain Gym, most of the children came out of their shock within a few days.

My experience in psychology and with these children has led me to understand how painful it can be for a child to be asked to explore a trauma when his mind and body are still in the first two stages of survival. I have found it to be of much greater benefit to first bring a child to a place that is internally safe, where protection and reactions are not necessary for survival. From this renewed perspective, a traumatized child is able to explore the story of his traumatic occurrence, moving into the stages of growth and development with a stronger sense of his own being.

As we have seen, if the mental exploration of a trauma is done prematurely, the mind and physiology are not in a place to support growth and development. The result can be that the experience of being stuck in a pattern of overprotection and overreaction leads down a dead-end street. These patterns can then become a vicious circle that may last for a lifetime.

When I walked into the children's ward and saw all the combined physical and emotional effects of extreme trauma, I knew I needed to find a tool I had never been given in school—

something that would allow the children to advance from their deeply rutted loops of survival to a safe present moment. As I've described, the Lazy 8s movement caught their attention first. Then the Double Doodle and Cross Crawl activities also attracted their curiosity as they joined me (either actually or in their imagination) in doing these developmental movements.

Now we were able to build a bridge from "there and then" to the "here and now." Once the children could actually cognize and experience that they were no longer stuck in the tragedy that had befallen them, they could begin building their resources of physical and mental strength. They learned to identify and release physiological reactions of survival and literally moved into the experience of feeling physically safe. From this position, they could now mentally "look" at fire and trauma with a new perception. Such is the gift of natural developmental movements in creating an environment for the safe release of mental reactions.

I knew that, in order to create long-lasting effects and to change their reactivity to the small details of the past, the children had to first see their future as a big picture. Only with the ability to see the whole picture from here and now would they feel safe enough to look back at what had happened. By awakening to the knowledge that they were winners, safely living in the present, they were able to change their perceptions about fire, trains, and travel. This became their foundation for moving forward without fear.

18. An Allegorical Tale

The use of story is a profound method of teaching because it stimulates the parts of the brain that allow us to paint our own picture within, relate and compare this knowledge with our own experiences, and then draw out our own learning from within. The essence of why Brain Gym worked so effectively with the children is shared here through the allegory of a story called "Phillip Goes to Braneland."

The characters in this story take us on a journey through the four complete and potential stages of the reflexive response to trauma.

Braneland is a play on the words "brain" and "land."

Phillip, a little boy, is the hero of our story.

Captain Pete represents the protective aspects of the freeze/flight mechanism of the brain stem. His command is to wear a suit of armor and stand very still, allowing the physiology to pause while the sensory system scans the environment, looking for danger.

General Vivian represents the limbic system's frantic and emotional call for fight or flight in order to move rapidly and escape any current danger.

The Land of Provival (a name that combines the words "protection" and "survival") is the place where Captain Pete and General Vivian live. This land is in the brain stem and/or the limbic system. Depression or anxiety are the trademarks of this land. In Provival, the body and mind are alert to the constant threat of perceived danger. The memory of a trauma continually reactivates the initial physiological survival strategies called upon during the earlier time of stress. From this angle of perception, the response to the past trauma will come from reaction. It is very easy to get stuck in the Land of Provival because of the repetition of old stories.

The Land of Nowgrow is a land of action instead of reaction. This kingdom is located in all parts of the cortex, working as a team with the rest of the brain. The left and right hemispheres working together (especially with the pre-frontal cortexes), consider the information coming in from the brain stem and limbic system and add in the gifts of logic, discrimination, reasoning, creativity, and emotional insight. In this land, one is able to be in the now moment. Here, reality is measured by the present moment rather than by the history of the past. This is the place where maturation and integration can spontaneously occur.

Prince Newton is a character who loves to investigate all things from new angles and perspectives. He delves into and plays with a variety of ways to experience sensori-motor events. Because of his willingness to pause and explore with curiosity, he is able to see new ways of looking at old problems. He is open to learning because he plays in the field of all possibilities.

Queen Della Mint represents the highest gifts—those that come when a reflex is fully integrated and anchored deeply within the body. Wisdom and clarity then reign. In 1929, Nikolai Bernstein wrote that movement is a natural gift to the person, and Queen Della Mint's name is a play on the word "development"—a playful way to honor these bountiful gifts.

Sir Wordson and Sir Reeceson are two characters whose names, again a play on words, are used to show that, when one is stuck in the lower areas of the brain, it can be challenging to hear words and reason. One must have clear connection with the cortex—especially the frontal and prefrontal lobes—for words and reasoning to make sense.

The Map of Braneland

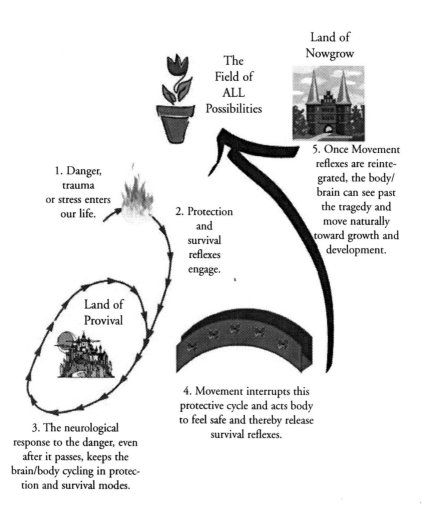

The
Field of
ALL
Possibilities

Land of
Nowgrow

1. Danger,
trauma
or stress enters
our life.

2. Protection
and
survival
reflexes
engage.

5. Once Movement
reflexes are reinte-
grated, the body/
brain can see past
the tragedy and
move naturally
toward growth and
development.

Land of
Provival

3. The neurological
response to the danger, even
after it passes, keeps the
brain/body cycling in protection and survival modes.

4. Movement interrupts this
protective cycle and acts body
to feel safe and thereby release
survival reflexes.

Phillip Goes to Braneland

Once upon a time, in a place called Braneland, there were two kingdoms: the Kingdom of Provival and the Kingdom of Nowgrow. The people of each kingdom had very important things to do, though each was very different.

The people of Provival had been taught for generations to protect Braneland from any danger. One of the soldiers from Provival was Captain Pete. He was strong and wore a shiny suit of armor covered with several dents. If he encountered any danger in Braneland it was his job to draw his sword and go to stop it.

Captain Pete's commanding officer was General Vivian. General Vivian kept the army and the kingdom of Provival ready to move. She believed the only way to survive danger was to stay two steps ahead of it, and so she ordered the people of Provival to keep their suitcases packed in case they needed to run.

Across the river, in the Kingdom of Nowgrow, things were very different. Her Majesty, Queen Della Mint had lived in Braneland longer than anyone and she felt very safe there. She spent time with her son, Prince Newton, exploring Braneland and learning about the wonderful things there. The people of Nowgrow were very wise.

One day, a boy came riding his pony as fast as he could intoBraneland. His home was far away to the south. He seemed very scared.

General Vivian, who was always on watch, noticed the boy first. She sent Captain Pete riding out to investigate. From a distant hilltop, Prince Newton was watching as Captain Pete stopped his horse in a clearing in the forest. Just then, the boy

Dr. Svetlana Masgutova & Pamela Curlee

and his pony rode out of the trees. Frightened by the sight of Captain Pete, the horse reared and bucked the boy off. The horse ran away back into the trees. The boy lay huddled on the ground, shaking.

"Who are you and what are you doing in Braneland?" yelled Captain Pete with his sword drawn.

"My name is Phillip," said the boy, but that was all he could say.

Captain Pete's eyes widened. He froze and sniffed the air. "Hark!" he cried, "There's danger! It's my job to protect you!"

He swept Phillip onto his horse and rode back to Provival.

Prince Newton was intrigued. He didn't see any danger anywhere, although it was clear something had frightened Phillip before he had arrived in Braneland. He walked home to tell Queen Della Mint what he had seen.

At the Provival castle, General Vivian had everyone in a stir. People were running about frantically. When Captain Pete entered the gates with Phillip, she hurried them along demanding to know what the danger was.

Phillip was too frightened to speak. He froze in his tracks, afraid to move farther. "No, no," said General Vivian, aghast, "We must keep moving, must keep moving. Everyone, hurry, hurry."

"Tell me, Phillip," said Captain Pete, "what danger follows you to Braneland?"

Phillip started crying. "There was a fire in my village," he began. "I woke up and there was smoke. I couldn't see. I crawled outside and jumped on my pony. We ran and ran but the fire was everywhere."

General Vivian shrieked. "Aaagh! Fire! A fire is coming! Call the bucket brigade! Bucket Brigade! Hurry! Fire is coming!

Move people! Move it, move it, move it!"

Phillip couldn't move. He just held on tightly to Captain Pete. The fire was following him!

General Vivian called to a soldier running past with a bucket slopping water. "Soldier, you must warn the Kingdom of Nowgrow. Tell them a fire is coming. We must be ready to run!"

In the palace of Nowgrow, Prince Newton had just finished telling Queen Della Mint about the boy when the messenger from Provival came running.

"Your Majesty, a message from General Vivian," he called. "A wildfire of historic proportions is coming! She urges Your Majesty to ready your kingdom to flee."

Queen Della Mint listened respectfully, but with a calm look said, "Thank you, messenger. You may return to Provival now, if you choose to."

The messenger dashed away.

Queen Della Mint reflected, "A wildfire coming towards us?" She looked to Prince Newton and other members of the Counsel who knew the truth.

Queen Della Mint surveyed the land. The sun was shining. The air smelled sweet like spring flowers. There was no fire coming. Although the court logbook showed there had been a fire far to the south several days ago, but a rainstorm had put it out.

The Counsel knew that the Provivalans had done the right thing by protecting the boy. However, in Provival there were no clocks, and so their fear of the danger could go on forever. The Counsel decided they had to rescue the boy from Provival and show him it was safe in Braneland.

The Counsel voted to send Sir Wordson and Sir Reeceson, who were wise and educated. The Counsel was certain that upon hearing their words, the people of Provival would gladly let Phillip go. So, the two knights set off and confidently marched up to the castle of Provival.

Phillip was curled up in a cold corner. Captain Pete had fashioned him a suit of armor much like his own. Every time he slept he had nightmares about fire. Even though Captain Pete stayed with him, he still didn't feel safe.

There was a knock on the door. Captain Pete drew his sword and swung the door open.

Sir Wordson and Sir Reeceson entered, looking past Captain Pete, and said to Phillip, "Hello, we're from the Kingdom of Nowgrow, across the river. We know that there was a fire in your village, but there are no fires now and there aren't any fires on the way. We want to take you to the Kingdom of Nowgrow to show you how wonderful Braneland is."

Phillip looked at the men as they spoke, but there was so much mayhem in the halls of the castle, people running about and yelling, that it was difficult for Phillip to hear anything they said.

Just then a screeching voice bellowed down the hallway, "What's the meaning of this?"

In came Dr. Riddle, a skinny man with wiry hair. He seemed very agitated.

"You gentlemen, what's the meaning of this, disturbing my patient?"

Sir Wordson explained who they were and that they wanted to take Phillip to Nowgrow where he would feel safe.

"Safe?" screeched Dr. Riddle, "Safe? Ha! The boy is terrified, and with good reason. The safest place for him is here, in my care."

"I respect your efforts, Doctor," said Sir Reeceson, "but we feel we can help the boy be less frightened and learn to enjoy the beauty of Braneland."

Dr. Riddle was stunned. He had never heard such talk as this in all his days. "I don't know what you think you can do that I haven't already done. The boy needs his potions. Without them he has nightmares and fits of panic. Now, good day to you gentlemen."

"But please, Doctor, if you'd just listen to Reeceson," argued Sir Wordson.

"Good day to you gentlemen," piped Dr. Riddle. "If you don't leave the castle at once I'll have you hung!"

Captain Pete stepped forward in front of Dr. Riddle, raising his sword.

The two knights had no choice but to leave.

Poor Phillip. He was stuck in this room, fearful of a fire that would never come. The potions Dr. Riddle gave just made him feel dizzy. Even with his armor, Captain Pete, and General Vivian there to protect him, he still didn't feel safe.

At Queen Della Mint's palace, the Counsel held a meeting. The Provivalans were working overtime and couldn't listen to Wordson and Reeceson. Something different had to be done.

"I have an idea," said Queen Della Mint, "Let's send Moovencat!"

Prince Newton had discovered a wonderful animal in Braneland, which he named Moovencat. While she looked like a regular orange tabby cat, she could do all sorts of interesting movements.

"Yes," they all agreed with enthusiasm, "we shall send Moovencat to invite Phillip to Nowgrow."

Outside Phillip's window he noticed an orange fl ash, like a bird, shaping a number 8 lying on its side. He was curious and went to the window. It wasn't a bird at all, but a cat, jumping in high circles like a streamer.

Moovencat landed on the ground outside the castle walls. She meowed to Phillip and then she marched around the grass on her hind legs, touching her front paws to the opposite legs like a dance.

Phillip laughed a little laugh. What a funny cat, he thought.

"Look, Captain Pete!" called Phillip. "The cat is dancing!"

Captain Pete came to the window and even he was intrigued.

"I'm going to go meet him," called Phillip, as he took off his armor and dashed out the door before Captain Pete could stop him. Phillip felt quite courageous. When he got outside the castle walls, he sat down with Moovencat. Moovencat showed him many more of her talents and Phillip even did some, too. He felt silly at first, but he liked Moovencat and trusted her.

Along came Dr. Riddle. "Phillip, it's time for your potions," he said.

"I don't want to take any potions. I'm feeling better today," Phillip said.

"What is this?" said Dr. Riddle, stunned. "Feeling better? Humph!" He stormed away to take up the matter with General Vivian.

Phillip hadn't even realized he'd left the safety of the castle. He noticed how frantic everyone in Provival was, and suddenly he thought how funny all the Provivalans looked, running about with their buckets of water.

Moovencat walked away toward the river and Phillip followed until they came to a bridge.

Standing on the other side of the bridge was Prince Newton.

"Hello, Phillip," he said. "I'm Prince Newton from the Kingdom of Nowgrow. Welcome to Braneland."

"I thought I was already in Braneland," Phillip responded.

"Yes," said Prince Newton, "but in Braneland there are two kingdoms, Provival and Nowgrow. As long as you are in Braneland, you have a choice about which kingdom you want to stay in."

"Is it safe in Nowgrow?" Phillip asked.

"You are close to Nowgrow. Does it feel safe to you?"

Phillip considered it for a moment. In fact, he did feel safe. He looked at Moovencat, who was meowing at Prince Newton's feet.

"Yes," Phillip said, but then he remembered General Vivian's warnings. "What about the fire?" he asked.

"There is no fire, Phillip."

"Oh yes there is," said Phillip, "there was a fire in my village. My house burned up. If it wasn't for my pony, I would have never escaped." He thought of running back to Provival.

"There was a fire, Phillip. But that happened in the past. In Nowgrow, we live for today. And today, there is no fire in Braneland, nor is there any fire coming this way. You are completely safe here."

Phillip looked around. A rainbow appeared in the field beyond the bridge. It did feel safe. He put one foot on the bridge, and then another. Moovencat ran across the bridge to meet him, so happy that he was coming to Nowgrow.

"Your pony has been here since you arrived in Braneland," said Prince Newton. "He'll be glad to have you back."

They went up to the palace of Nowgrow where Queen Della Mint and the other members of the Counsel welcomed him.

"Tell me, Phillip, how do you like Nowgrow?" she asked.

"It feels very safe," he answered.

"Yes, it does," replied Queen Della Mint. "Do you know why?"

"Because of Moovencat?"

"Partly," said Queen Della Mint. "but also because Provival rules the Land of the Past. Since the fire scared you in the past, sometimes you may feel like you need to go back to Provival to be protected. Here, we live in the Land of Now. In Nowgrow, you can see what is real at this moment. As long as you are in Braneland, it's your choice whether you want to live in Nowgrow or go back to Provival. What do you say to that?"

"I would like to stay here, in Nowgrow," said Phillip.

Queen Della Mint smiled. Then she lifted up a beautiful candle.

Phillip trembled for a moment. The sight of the flame reminded him of the fire in his village.

That was in the past, he thought. Here he felt safe and brave, and he could see that today the fire was small and cast a pretty light in the room. He imagined the fire in his village being as small as the flame on the candlestick. He could blow it out with a puff.

"Good," said Queen Della Mint. "In Nowgrow, you can see things that frightened you in a new way. You can change their color, sounds and smell and even how they make you feel. Its part of the choices you make!"

Phillip stayed for a long time, but he missed his family. He asked Queen Della Mint what would happen when he left Braneland.

Queen Della Mint answered, "You are never very far from Braneland. If you need us, we will always be here. Come visit as often as you like."

When Captain Pete and General Vivian heard that Phillip was going home and that there was no fire, they began to relax and the people of Provival returned to their watchtowers, ready to serve another day.

All the people of Nowgrow came out to say good-bye to Phillip. Prince Newton gave Moovencat to Phillip to go with him.

Phillip rode his pony home and found the houses had been rebuilt and the village looked even nicer than before. Phillip told his family all about Braneland, and how he had become so brave. He was a hero. His stories went on long into the night, until finally, Phillip safely fell asleep by the warm glowing coals in the hearth.

THE END

And so, dear reader, we invite you to notice when and if you find yourself captured by Captain Pete or General Vivian. If you are living in the Land of Provival, you may find yourself repeating old stories and feeling as if your only defense is to dig a trench into the ground as you continue feeling that you need protection or that you're a victim.

We also invite you to move with the Brain Gym activities, which are just like the dances of Moovencat. You will naturally begin to experience the peace and safety of living in the Land of Nowgrow. From these higher levels of your brain, you'll naturally begin to have a new perspective and understanding of who you are now. We celebrate the *winner* within you awakening to this expanded awareness and to the field of all possibilities.

19. You, Too, Are a *Winner!*

You, too, dear reader, are a *winner!* No matter what crisis you have endured, you are a *winner!* Do you know how I know? I'll show you. Come. Look.

There are trillions of thoughts, and out of these trillions, one inspired thought imagined you. This one unique thought had your name on it, and you won!

Do you know how special you are? I'll show you. Come. Look.

Once upon a time, millions of racers were participating in the creation marathon. At the end of this race, the *winner* was to be given the honor of conception. Only one of the racers could win. Out of millions of racers, the most special one crossed the finish line first. This champion was welcomed and embraced. You were created. You won again! Do you see how amazing that is? I'll show you. Come. Look.

Celebration! It was your day of birth. You encountered many obstacles, and yet you met each barrier with determination and reached for Life. Once again, you were successful. You overcame each obstacle with your natural wisdom. You won! Do you know how inspiring you are? You will show us. We will come. We will see.

You are exceptional. You're a *winner!* You have proven it. And you will go on winning.

ABOUT THE AUTHORS

Svetlana Masgutova, Ph.D. is a world-renowned Psychologist and Neuro Kinesiologist.

She is the Founder of the International Dr. Svetlana Masgutova Instituteâ, in Warsaw, Poland and the Svetlana Masgutova Educational Institute for Neuro-Sensory-Motor and Reflex Integration in the US. She has been an International Faculty member of the Educational Kinesiology Foundation/ *Brain Gym®* International Program since 1994. Her scientific research on Brain Gym and Neuro Kinesiology has been published in over 70 professional journals in Russia and Poland. She has created a training program for Neuro Kinesiology that she teaches around the world. Her work profoundly impacts the lives of people by enriching emotional, mental, and physical potentials.

Pamela Curlee, co-author of *Trauma Recovery—You Are A Winner,* has been an International Faculty member of the Educational Kinesiology Foundation/*Brain Gym®* International Program since 1990. She has been a consultant and instructor in Brain Gym since 1984. She is also the creator and founder of the Switched-On Golf® program. She became an International Facutly for the Svetlana Masgutova Educational Institute for Neuro-Sensory-Motor and Reflex Integration in 2005. She brings the joy of learning and self discovery to a variety of Brain Gym and NeuroKinesiology classes that she teaches around the world.

Printed in the United States
90469LV00005B/22/A

9 781421 899558